GUIDE TO GERMANY

MICHAEL MARCH

Highlights for Children

CONTENTS

On the cover: A view of the town of Cochem and its church on the Mosel River in the west of Germany, with a historic *burg*, or castle, in the foreground.

The publisher is grateful for the assistance of Anika Kiehne in reviewing this book. Ms. Kiehne is a doctoral candidate at the Department of Germanic Languages and Literatures at the University of Pennsylvania. Originally from Kiel, Germany, where she received a degree in German, English, and Pedagogy, Ms. Kiehne's research interests include late eighteenth- and early nineteenth-century German women authors.

Published by Highlights for Children
© 1996 Highlights for Children, Inc.
P.O. Box 18201
Columbus, Ohio 43218-0201
For information on *Top Secret Adventures*, visit www.tsadventures.com or call 1-800-962-3661.

10 9 8
ISBN 0-87534-926-9

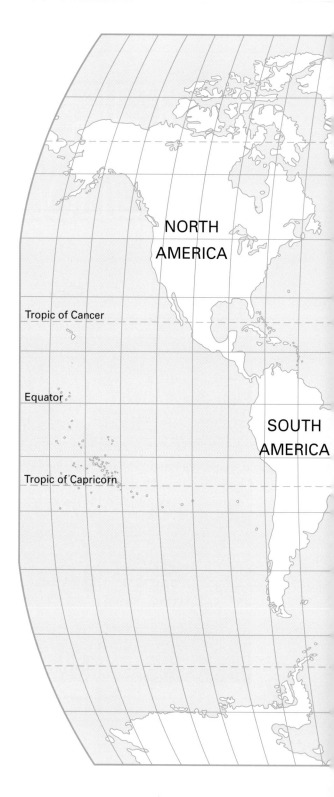

Germany
EUROPE

ASIA

AFRICA

AUSTRALIA

ANTARCTICA

△ **The German flag**
Germany's flag has
been black, red, and
gold since the early
19th century. When
the country was
divided in 1949, West
Germany used this
flag. Today Germany is
a single country again,
and once again this is
the national flag.

3

GERMANY AT A GLANCE

Area 137,820 square miles (356,733 square kilometers)

Population 82,400,996

Capital Berlin, population 3,404,037

Other big cities Hamburg (1,754,182), Munich (1,294,608)

Highest mountain Zugspitze, 9,720 feet (2,963 meters)

Longest river Rhine, section in Germany 436 miles (698 kilometers)

Largest lake Lake Constance (Bodensee), part in Germany 119 square miles (305 square kilometers)

Official language German

▽ **German postage stamps** Two show German architecture and a food market. Others celebrate a country women's association, the 100th anniversary of the Wuppertal suspension railway, and the 150th anniversary of the Leonhard pilgrimage.

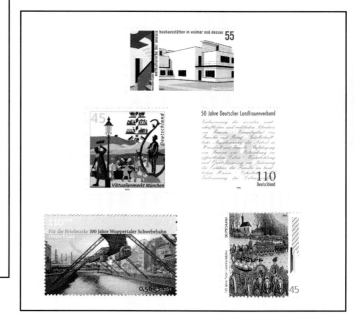

◁ **German money** The currency of the Federal Republic of Germany is the euro (€). The country belongs to the European Union (EU) and has the same currency as other EU member countries. For example, this 10-euro note could be used in France or Ireland.

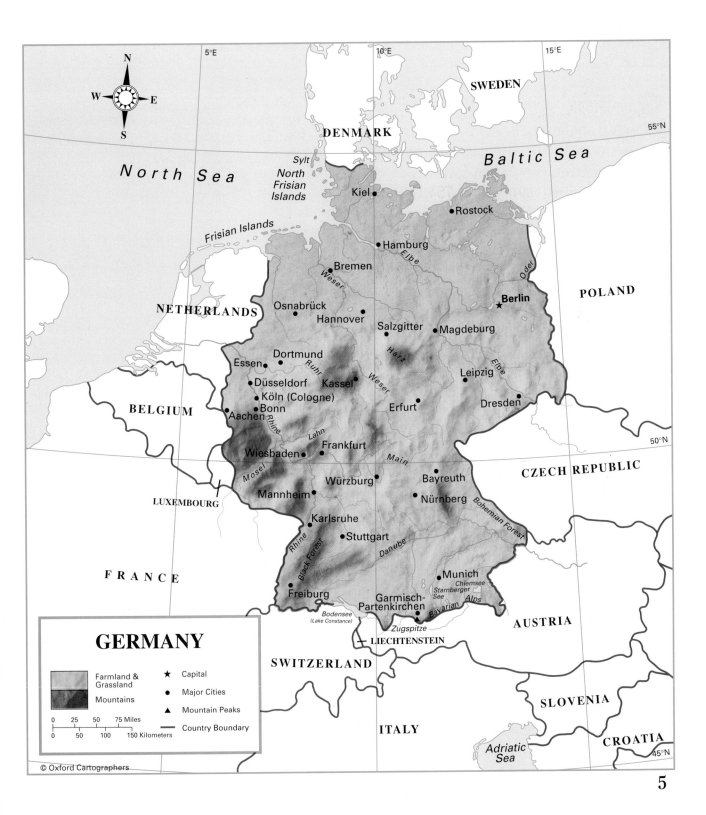

N

W E

S

5°E

10°E

15°E

55°N

North Sea

Baltic Sea

SWEDEN

DENMARK

Sylt
North Frisian Islands

Kiel •

• Rostock

Frisian Islands

• Hamburg

Elbe

• Bremen

Weser

NETHERLANDS

Osnabrück •

Hannover •

Salzgitter •

• Magdeburg

★ **Berlin**

Oder

POLAND

Dortmund •

Essen •

Ruhr

Harz

• Leipzig

Elbe

Düsseldorf •

Kassel •

Weser

Köln (Cologne) •

Bonn •

Aachen •

Erfurt •

• Dresden

BELGIUM

Rhine

Lahn

Wiesbaden •

• Frankfurt

Main

CZECH REPUBLIC

50°N

Mosel

Würzburg •

Bayreuth •

LUXEMBOURG

Mannheim •

Nürnberg •

Bohemian Forest

Karlsruhe •

• Stuttgart

Danube

FRANCE

Rhine

Black Forest

• Munich

Chiemsee
Starnberger See

Freiburg •

Garmisch-Partenkirchen •

Bavarian Alps

Bodensee
(Lake Constance)

▲ *Zugspitze*

AUSTRIA

⊢ LIECHTENSTEIN

SWITZERLAND

SLOVENIA

ITALY

Adriatic Sea

CROATIA

45°N

GERMANY

Farmland & Grassland

Mountains

★ Capital

• Major Cities

▲ Mountain Peaks

— Country Boundary

0   25   50   75 Miles

0   50   100   150 Kilometers

© Oxford Cartographers

5

AT THE HEART OF EUROPE

Germany lies in the center of the continent of Europe. It extends from Denmark in the north to Switzerland and Austria in the south. Germany shares borders with nine other countries and has coasts on the North and Baltic Seas. The country's full name is the Federal Republic of Germany.

Northern Germany is mostly flat. The south has beautiful scenery. From the south, the Danube River, Europe's second-longest river, begins its long journey eastward. The Rhine River flows northward from Lake Constance on the Swiss border. In Germany it can rain in any season, and in winter it snows. Sometimes the Baltic Sea freezes over. But spring comes early to the south because of a warm wind, called the *Föhn*. This wind blows down from the Alps mountains and warms the land.

For much of its history, Germany has not been a single country. Many of its beautiful old castles, palaces, and churches were built by kings and princes who ruled separate territories. More recently Germany was two countries, called West Germany and East Germany. In 1990, after forty years of separation, the two Germanies were reunited.

Today more than 80 million people live in Germany, more than in any other European country except Russia. They include Turks and other immigrants who live and work in Germany. The German people have their own language and one of the world's richest cultures. Many of the greatest composers, writers, philosophers, and scientists are German. You can explore this exciting country by train or by car on Europe's fastest roads. There is no speed limit on a German *Autobahn* (superhighway).

▷ **Olympic Stadium, Munich** The 1972 Summer Olympic Games were held here. The Olympic tower is 960 feet (290 meters) high and gives a good view over Munich and the Alps.

6

◁ **Fruit and vegetable market in Mainz, western Germany** The market square of this old city on the Rhine was built in the Middle Ages.

▽ **Schloss Linderhof** This fine palace was built for King Ludwig II of Bavaria more than a hundred years ago. Bavaria, once a separate kingdom, is in southern Germany.

THE OLD CAPITAL

Germany's historic capital city, Berlin, lies on the Spree River, in the northeastern part of the country. Berlin grew out of a small fishing village in the Middle Ages and was the capital of the old kingdom of Prussia from 1701 to 1871. During this period, it became a cultural center. At Charlottenburg Palace with its magnificent dome you can visit the apartments where the Prussian kings used to spend their summers.

Berlin became the national capital in 1871 when Germany was united under Prussian rule. It remained the country's most important city for more than seventy years. In 1945, at the end of World War II, Germany was defeated and then divided into two countries—West Germany and East Germany. Berlin, which was the capital of the new communist-controlled East Germany, was also split into East and West.

▽ **View over east Berlin from the west** The Spree River is on the left. In the distance is the Fernsehturm (Television Tower), one of the city's most famous landmarks.

In 1961 the East Germans built a concrete wall 13 feet (4 meters) high around their part of the city, with special crossing points to West Berlin. The wall was to prevent East Berliners from leaving for West Germany. Now there are no communist governments in Europe. The wall has been knocked down. All Germans can travel around freely. You may find pieces of the wall being sold here as souvenirs.

In downtown Berlin you can relax in the Tiergarten, a lovely wooded park with lakes. "Tiergarten" means "animal garden." On the southwestern edge of the park you will find a large, well-planned zoo.

You can get around using the subway, trains, or buses. In the eastern part of the city there are trams. Shopping and eating out are fun, and you can enjoy music played by some of the world's greatest orchestras.

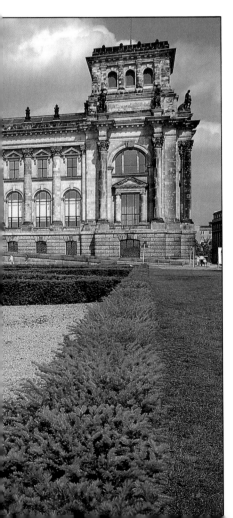

◁ **The Reichstag, Berlin** The building was designed more than a hundred years ago to house the German parliament. It was damaged in World War II but was repaired in 1969.

▽ **The Kurfürstendamm, Berlin** Shops, restaurants, and cafés line this busy street. It is overlooked by the Kaiser Wilhelm Memorial Church, a famous Berlin ruin.

GOING EAST

At the very heart of Berlin, east of the Tiergarten, is the Brandenburg Gate. The huge stone gateway is Berlin's proudest monument. Today you can pass through the Brandenburg Gate to the famous Unter den Linden street. Its central island is shaded by linden trees, which are sometimes called lime trees, and which give the street its name. *Unter den Linden* is German for "under the lime trees."

At the end of the trees is a 44-foot (14 meter)-high statue of the Prussian king Frederick the Great. He was crowned in Berlin in 1740 and made the city a center of learning. Opposite the statue is the old Humboldt University. The great scientist Albert Einstein and the brothers Jakob and Wilhelm Grimm, known for their work with folk tales, are among the famous people who once taught here.

There are many beautiful churches, museums, and squares in East Berlin. Some of them are more than two hundred years old. They contrast with more modern buildings such as the Fernsehturm (TV Tower) on the square called Alexanderplatz.

◁ **Booksellers outside Humboldt University** A statue of Wilhelm von Humboldt stands in front of the university named after him. The fine building was used as a palace by Frederick the Great's brother before Humboldt made it into a university in 1809.

▷ **Brandenburg Gate** This famous monument is more than 200 years old. On top is a statue of the Goddess of Victory in her chariot.

▷ **Gendarmenmarkt, one of Berlin's finest squares** The cathedral was built in the 18th century for French Protestant settlers.

The Fernsehturm's revolving platform is 680 feet (207 meters) above the ground and gives a fine view over the city. To the south are the cafés and kebab stalls of the Turkish quarter. A large lake, the Müggelsee, lies in the distance to the southeast.

A short train ride from Berlin will take you to Potsdam, a town surrounded by woods and lakes. Frederick the Great built the most famous palace in Potsdam. Its name is Sanssouci, which is French for "carefree." Here, away from the bustle of the capital, the king entertained his friends.

CULTURE AND RELIGION

Traveling southwest from Berlin, you can enjoy the beautiful scenery of the old region of Saxony. Take a ride through the Harz mountains on the famous narrow-gauge steam railroad. You can also visit some lovely old towns with traditional "half-timbered" houses. These houses have plaster or brick walls set in a wooden frame.

The Bauhaus building in the little town of Dessau looks quite different. It is made of concrete, steel, and enormous amounts of glass. Walter Gropius, a German architect, designed the Bauhaus in the 1920s. Since then, this style of building has been copied all over the world.

Not far from Dessau is another little town, Wittenberg. Here, hundreds of years ago, a monk named Martin Luther was unhappy with the ways of the Catholic Church in Rome. Luther founded a new form of Christianity, the Protestant movement, which then spread across Europe. You can visit Luther's house and the church where he nailed up his list of complaints against the Church of Rome.

To the south is the big, busy city of Leipzig. The great composer Johann Sebastian Bach is buried here in St. Thomas's church, where he was once the organist. Another great composer, Robert Schumann, lived at Zwickau, a town farther south. Schumann's house is now a museum.

One of Germany's most famous cultural cities is Weimar, on the Ilm River. In the eighteenth century some of the country's finest artists and writers lived here. They included Johann Wolfgang von Goethe and Friedrich Schiller, two of Germany's greatest poets. There is a statue of them in front of the National Theater.

▷ **A scene in "Saxon Switzerland"** This is the name given to the rocky highlands above the valley of the Elbe River, near Germany's border with the Czech Republic.

◁ **The market square, Halle** Church spires rise above the old square, where streetcars come and go.

▽ **Tour boats on the Elbe River, below Meissen's Domberg** Meissen, in Saxony, is famous for its porcelain.

MOUNTAINS AND CASTLES

Germany is made up of sixteen states, or *Länder*. The biggest of these is Bavaria, in the southern part of the country. Bavaria was a separate kingdom until 1918, nearly fifty years after the rest of Germany was united. Here you will find storybook castles, lakes, forests, and pretty mountain villages. You may see men with traditional goatee beards and leather shorts called *Lederhosen*. Women may be seen wearing *Dirndls*, frilly outfits with embroidered skirts.

Bavaria's lovely capital, Munich, lies on the banks of the Isar River, within sight of the Alps. It is Germany's third-largest city. The Bavarian Motor Works, maker of BMW cars, is located here.

The heart of the city is the old market square, called Marienplatz. Street musicians and artists come here to entertain the many tourists. Munich's huge Town Hall building dominates the square. From the viewing gallery on the clock tower you can get a good view over the city and surroundings. Twice a day, mechanical dolls on the tower dance and rotate as the clock chimes. The German name for this is the *Glockenspiel*.

▷ **Munich Town Hall** Below the clock is the Glockenspiel.

Behind the Town Hall you can see the onion domes on the towers of the Church of Our Lady. The old church, which stands in a square by itself, is a famous city landmark. The stained-glass windows look beautiful when sunlight shines in through them.

During the winter the Bavarian Alps are popular with skiers. In summer they attract hikers. A cable car will take you to the top of Germany's highest mountain, the Zugspitze. Looking west from here, you can see the Allgäu highlands, where farmers produce some of Germany's finest cheeses.

◁ **A parade of children in traditional dress during Oktoberfest** The Oktoberfest is Munich's famous beer festival. It lasts for sixteen days, ending on the first Sunday in October.

▷ **Neuschwanstein Castle, Bavaria** King Ludwig II's storybook castle is in front of the mountains near the old town of Füssen. It was designed, not by an architect, but by a theater set designer. It was never completed.

Lakes, Rivers, and Forests

Beautiful Lake Constance is Germany's biggest lake. It forms part of the borders with Switzerland and Austria. The Rhine River enters Germany through the lake.

On the banks of Lake Constance, apples, pears, and grapes ripen in the sun. There are wooded hills and pretty lakeside towns and villages to visit.

The longest river flowing through Germany is the Danube, or "Donau" in German. In the town of Donaueschingen you can see the spring where the river begins. It flows across Europe to the Black Sea 1,800 miles (2,900 kilometers) away.

Donaueschingen lies on the edge of an enormous dark forest. Fir, oak, and beech trees cover the hillsides. This is the famous Black Forest. Here, craftsmen still make cuckoo clocks and blow glass over wood-heated furnaces. You can take a thrilling train ride through the forest. The train travels up steep mountains, around sharp bends, and through tunnels in the rocks.

Freiburg im Breisgau has been called "the capital of the Black Forest." The town is known for its old university and the dark-red sandstone cathedral with soaring spires.

To the north is Heidelberg, another old university town. Its best-known monument is the ruins of an old castle that stand on a hillside overlooking the Neckar River.

The big city of Stuttgart, in the region called Swabia, is the home of the world-famous Porsche and Mercedes-Benz cars. There you can visit the manufacturers' motor museums and join a guided tour of the Porsche production line.

◁ **Black Forest** A little hamlet with red-tiled roofs nestles in a valley near the small town of Wolfach in the Kinzig Valley.

◁ **The marina at Meersburg** This little town lies on the northern shore of Lake Constance. Frequent ferries cross the lake from here to the largest lakeside town, Konstanz, near the Swiss border.

▽ **Mercedes–Benz production line, Stuttgart** This is the world's oldest car factory. The first Mercedes was built here in 1901.

BUSINESS AND TRADE

Frankfurt am Main is Germany's most modern city. Tall office buildings alongside the Main River remind visitors of New York City. The 53-story Messeturm is one of Germany's most recognizable landmarks. It is in Frankfurt's Messegelände (Trade Fair Grounds), site of a world-famous book fair.

Frankfurt has been a major trading center for more than 800 years. Hundreds of German and foreign businesses are based in the city. Germany's national bank, the Bundesbank, has its headquarters here. The city is sometimes called "Mainhatten" because of its many banks and high skyline.

Frankfurt is also a major hub of Germany's road and rail networks and has the second-busiest international airport in Europe. Airplanes from all over the world take off and land here daily. Many are flown by Lufthansa, the German National Airline.

The oldest part of Frankfurt is the Römerberg square, near the river. Long ago, Europe's Holy Roman Emperors were crowned in the cathedral here.

▷ **Frankfurt am Main** The oldest part of Germany's most modern city lies along the river.

△ **Frankfurt Stock Exchange** Shares worth billions of euros are traded here every year.

▷ **Passengers at Frankfurt railroad station** ICE (InterCity Express) trains run between the major cities at up to 175 miles (280 kilometers) per hour.

Marburg, farther north, is a lovely old town of narrow winding streets built on a hillside. It overlooks the Lahn River and is crowned by a fine fifteenth-century castle. The tale of Little Red Riding Hood came from near here. On special occasions villagers dress up and act out the story.

Wiesbaden, to the west of Frankfurt, is a famous health resort town. Since the last century, many people have traveled here to enjoy the hot spring waters. Some also like to try their luck in the casinos.

DOWN THE RHINE

Opposite the old town of Mainz, the Main River flows into the Rhine. In the Middle Ages, the bishops of Mainz were powerful. Some of them are buried in fine tombs in Mainz's great cathedral on the market square. Cross the square and you come to the Gutenberg Museum. During the 1450s, Johannes Gutenberg of Mainz became the first European to print from moveable type. The museum houses Gutenberg's first printed Bible and a full-size model of his printing press.

Long, narrow barges glide up and down the Rhine River. They carry goods to and from northern Europe. Because of this trade, the Rhine has always been Germany's most important river. The best way to see the Rhine is to cruise down the river on a steamship. Ahead lies the spectacular Rhine Gorge. Here, the river bends left and right between steep wooded banks. Fields of grapes cover the lower slopes. Pretty villages with half-timbered houses nestle in the hillsides. From high up on the cliff tops, romantic old castles look down on the river below.

One of the Rhine's most famous sights is the huge Lorelei rock, which rises to 433 feet (132 meters) on the right bank of the river. A famous legend tells how a young woman once sat here combing her hair and the sound of her singing lured ships onto the rocks.

Like the Rhine Valley, the valley of the Mosel River produces many good wines. Germany's oldest city, Trier, lies in the Mosel Valley. The Porta Nigra (Black Gate), which once marked the entrance to the city, is one of Europe's finest Roman buildings. It is made of huge sandstone blocks held together by iron bolts. It is now black with age.

▷ **Chair lift on the Rhine Gorge** Below is Assmannshausen, a pretty village known for its red wine. A long barge makes its way up the Rhine River in the background.

▷ **Shopping for meat and sausages** German sausages, called *Würste*, are famous all over the world.

△ **Gau Street in Mainz** The dome of the old St. Stephen's Church can be seen behind the other buildings.

GOVERNMENT AND INDUSTRY

When West Germany was a separate country, its capital was Bonn. The town was founded by the Romans, but it never grew to be a large city like its neighbor Cologne.

The composer Ludwig van Beethoven was born in Bonn. Beethoven wrote some of the best-loved music of all time. His house in the old town district is now a museum.

From Bonn you can see forest-covered mountains on the opposite bank of the Rhine. They are the Siebenbirge, where the Grimm brothers' folk story *Snow White* is supposed to have taken place.

To the north of Bonn lies Cologne. Approaching Cologne by train across the Hohenzollern Bridge gives a fine view of the city. Cologne's magnificent cathedral is made of stone that was taken from the Siebengebirge. It was built to house the Shrine of the Magi (the Three Wise Men in the Christmas story). Building began in 1248 but did not finish until 600 years later.

At the start of spring, the people of Cologne hold their carnival. On Shrove Monday, young and old dress up and join in street parades. Musicians, horses, and colorful floats accompany them.

North of Cologne lies the Ruhrgebiet region. Here, in the last century, big towns grew up as the coal and steel industries developed. The world's biggest inland port is at Duisburg, a steelmaking city on the Ruhr River. Today, many of the mines have been closed and the land turned into green fields. Pigeon racing is a favorite pastime of the people who live in the Ruhrgebiet.

◁ **Half-timbered houses at Monschau** This pretty town lies in the Eifel Mountains, near the border with Belgium. Black-and-white mansions with slate roofs line the riverbanks.

▽ **A sidewalk artist and tourists outside Cologne Cathedral** The cathedral stands near the west bank of the Rhine River. It is one of Europe's largest churches.

△ **Christmas shopping by Aachen Cathedral** Aachen is Germany's westernmost city. The eight-sided tower is nearly 1,200 years old. The remains of the emperor Charlemagne, who ruled much of Europe from 771 to 814, are kept here.

THE NORTHWEST

Hannover has been called the "city in the country." Gardens, fountains, a deer park, forests, and lakes—you will find them all here.

Three hundred years ago Gottfried Wilhelm Leibniz, a great philosopher and mathematician, lived in Hannover. You can visit Leibniz's tomb in the Neustädter Church, near the east bank of the Leine River. Today Hannover is known for its industrial trade fair, which is held here every spring.

Hameln, a town that used to be called Hamelin, to the southwest, was the setting for Robert Browning's famous poem *The Pied Piper of Hamelin*. The poem is based on the legend of a musician who rid the town of rats in the 1280s. Every Sunday during spring and summer, near the market square, actors in costumes perform the Pied Piper story.

▽ **Sidewalk cafés in Hameln** The historic town on the Weser River has many lovely old buildings.

▽ **Bremerhaven** Old ships that belong to the German Shipping Museum collection stand in the harbor.

Wolfsburg, to the east of Hannover, is the home of Volkswagen, one of Europe's biggest car makers. The car factory started here in the 1930s. The town grew up around it. The famous Volkswagen "Beetle" was made in Wolfsburg for twenty years. It became the most popular car ever.

Germany's oldest port is Bremen, on the Weser River. Ships carrying cargoes of tobacco, cotton, and coffee have passed through here for hundreds of years. Outside the town hall there is a huge statue of the city's hero, Roland. This statue has represented the freedom of Bremen since 1404.

At the mouth of the Weser River, on the North Sea, lies Bremerhaven. It is Europe's biggest fishing port. Sometimes you can see fish being sold by auction on the wharf. The northern end of the port has huge docks for container ships.

▽ **Bright lights in downtown Kassel** This modern city south of Hannover is famous for its art galleries and museums.

THE GERMAN COAST

Visiting Hamburg, you would not think it was Germany's second-biggest city. Only one-third of it is built up. The rest of it is parks and gardens, and lakes and canals crossed by bridges. Hamburg lies near the mouth of the Elbe River, 55 miles (90 kilometers) from the North Sea. It is Germany's biggest seaport, with more than thirty docks and hundreds of docking spaces for ships.

The warehouse district, with its cobblestone streets, is a fascinating old place. Some of the red brick warehouses lining the wharfs are seven stories high. All kinds of goods are stored here—from tea, spices, and Oriental carpets to televisions and computers. Because the buildings are so old, no lifting machines are allowed. Using hooks and pulleys, dockworkers must move everything by hand.

To the west of Hamburg, the marshy Altes Land (Old Country) is a major fruit-growing region. It is seen at its best in spring when the cherry trees are in bloom. If you like wild scenery and fresh sea air, fly from Hamburg to Helgoland, a rugged island out in the North Sea. Or you can take a boat to the Frisian Islands off the North Sea coast.

One of the world's busiest shipping canals crosses northern Germany, linking the North Sea with the Baltic Sea. Here, on the Baltic coast, you can swim from sandy beaches overlooked by chalk cliffs or woodlands and explore old fishing villages. Some local people collect amber from the seabed and make it into jewelry. The center of the amber trade is near the big port of Rostock. Inland, you will find hills with hundreds of lakes among forests and farmland. This is a beautiful place to end your tour of Germany.

▷ **Feeding the swans in Hamburg** Foreign embassy buildings and fine houses look out over Hamburg's lakes and canals.

▽ **The port of Hamburg** Pleasure boats touring the port leave from St. Pauli pier. Steinwerder island, where ships are loaded and unloaded, is a mass of cranes.

◁ **Travemünde, a Baltic coast resort** Basket chairs protect beach-goers from the wind.

GERMANY FACTS AND FIGURES

People

Most German people are descended from Germanic tribes who appeared in Europe about 2,800 years ago. The Germans are closely related to the Austrians and Swiss, and less closely to the English and Scandinavians.

Since 1945, many people from other countries have settled in Germany.

△ **A street in Garmisch-Partenkirchen, in the Bavarian Alps** This beautiful old painted building has an overhanging roof typical of Alpine houses.

Trade and Industry

Germany is one of the world's major trading nations. Much of the country's wealth comes from manufacturing and mining. Germany produces more lignite (brown coal) than any country, except the United States. But most of the oil and natural gas needed to supply Germany's electricity has to be imported. Some German electricity power stations use hydroelectricity (from dams on rivers), nuclear energy, or wind energy.

Steel is needed for Germany's great car-making industry and for building ships. Most iron ore, used in the making of steel, is also bought from other countries.

Germany also produces trucks, machinery, electrical goods, chemicals, paper, and wood pulp.

Farming

About a third of Germany is planted with crops. These include sugar beets, from which refined sugar is made, as well as wheat, rye, and other grains. Farmers also grow potatoes, cabbages, and other vegetables, and fruits such as apples, strawberries, and black currants. Hops, from which the country's 5,000 kinds of beer are made, are a very important crop. So too are the wine-making grapes of the Rhine and Mosel valleys.

Elsewhere, dairy cattle provide the country with butter, milk, and cheese, while beef cattle and pigs are kept for their meat.

Many German farms are small and operated part time by farmers who have other jobs.

Fishing

Germany's large fishing fleets trawl the North Sea, the Baltic Sea, and Atlantic and Pacific Oceans. Bremerhaven is Europe's largest fishing port. The catch includes herring, haddock, plaice, skate, cod, and Rotbarsch (rosefish).

Lake Constance (Bodensee) has carp, pike, sander, trout, and perch, as well as unusual freshwater types such as giant catfish.

Food

Many German dishes, including the famous sausages known as *Würste*, are made with pork. Here are some regional dishes:

Bavaria: *Krautwickerl*—white cabbage stuffed with minced beef *Gugelhupf*—yeast cake made with almonds and raisins

Saxony: *Galbertschüssel*—boiled pig's feet in aspic

Rhineland: *Sauerbraten*—braised pickled beef

Northern Germany: *Lübecker Schwalbennester*—a rolled slice of veal stuffed with mashed hard-boiled egg

Rote Grütze—Raspberry pudding

Northeastern Germany: *Salzhering in Sahnesosse*—pickled herring in sour cream

Schools

Schooling in Germany is free and standards are high. All children must attend school. Most spend four years at elementary school, followed by five or six years at high school. They may then stay for another three years to prepare for the examination known as the *Abitur*, or they can begin training for a job. Students who pass the Abitur may continue to study at a university or a college. Germany has some of the world's best universities.

The Media

Germany has more than 350 daily newspapers. Most of them are regional but some, such as the *Frankfurter Allgemeine Zeitung* are read nationally. There are also many magazines, covering everything from current affairs to fashion and sports.

The two main television channels, ARD and ZDF, broadcast to all of Germany. ARD comprises all the regional broadcasting systems, including several *Dritte Programme* (Third Programs), which present educational programs. German radio includes stations that broadcast in English.

△ **A selection of German breads** They include white, brown, and black rye bread, and rolls seasoned with caraway, sesame, or poppy seeds.

Literature and Drama

There have been many great German novelists, poets, and playwrights. The most famous is Johann Wolfgang von Goethe (1749–1832). His best-known work is the drama *Faust*. Also well known are the folk stories collected in the 1800s by brothers Jakob and Wilhelm Grimm.

Thomas Mann (1875–1955) wrote novels and short stories about society and the place of the artist within it. Bertolt Brecht (1898–1956), in his plays and novels, criticized rich people and called for an end to all war.

More recent famous German writers include the novelists Günter Grass (1927–) and Heinrich Böll (1917–1985).

Art

In the 16th century, the German artists Albrecht Dürer and Lucas Cranach produced great paintings, woodcuts, and copperplate engravings. They painted mainly portraits or religious subjects.

Twentieth century German artists introduced many new ideas. In 1919, Walter Gropius set up the Bauhaus school to bring together art, architecture, and design. Max Ernst helped start the Surrealist movement in 1924. Käthe Kollwitz (1867–1945) made woodcuts and sculptures showing the misery caused by war and poverty.

Music

The works of Bach, Beethoven, Wagner, and other German composers are heard all over the world. Johann Sebastian Bach (1685–1750) wrote works for voices, harpsichord, and organ. He also wrote the Brandenburg Concertos for full orchestra. Even better known are the symphonies and piano concertos of Ludwig van Beethoven. Richard Wagner (1813–1883) wrote vast operas that combined music, drama, and poetry in a new way.

GERMANY FACTS AND FIGURES

Religion

Germany has no official religion. Traditionally, Germans are Christians. Those in the north of the country are mostly Protestant, while southern Germans and those living in the Rhineland are mostly Catholics. Settlers from abroad include Christians and Muslims.

Festivals and Holidays

Christmas Day and New Year's Day are national holidays. Some religious celebrations are public holidays only in Catholic regions. Festivals are an important part of the German way of life. They range from international to local events. Here is a selection:

30 April **Walpurgisnacht** (Witches' Sabbath) held in the Harz and Saxony-Anhalt. People attend parties dressed as witches and monsters.

July **Überlingen**, on Lake Constance. A festival of traditional sword dances in the town hall

July–August **Bayreuth**, Bavaria. A celebration of the music of Richard Wagner

August **Rhein in Flammen**, in Koblenz. Spectacular firework displays on the Rhine

△ **Drachenstich festival, Furth im Wald, Bavaria** Every August, hundreds of people turn out to celebrate St. George's victory over the Dragon.

Sports

For a long time, young Germans have been encouraged to play and take an interest in sports. German soccer players, tennis players, and field and track athletes are among the best in the world. Soccer is the sport that is most enjoyed by spectators in Germany. Car racing also has a strong following, and horse shows and horse racing have their fans, too.

In winter, the German Alps attract skiing enthusiasts. In summer, keen surfers head for the coastal resorts. Fishing is also popular on the coasts and on lakes and rivers inland.

Other popular sports include volleyball, basketball, squash, cycling, and jogging.

Plants

About a third of Germany is woodland. Mountainous regions are covered with spruce, pine, or silver fir trees. Bilberries, ferns, and mosses grow beneath some trees. On the lower mountain slopes, beech, elm, maple, linden, ash, and oak trees are found.

The low North German Plain is mostly farming land, but includes pockets of heath, moor, and bog. Here, purple heather grows alongside mosses and lichens and, in some places, with juniper bushes.

Animals

Germany's forests are home to many roe and red deer, pine martens, and wildcats. Hundreds of thousands of birds nest and breed in the marshes and mudflats of Germany's North Sea coast. These include the rare sandwich tern, as well as the cormorant, which feeds on crabs, worms, and mollusks in the mud.

Forest birds, such as the rare capercaillie and hazel grouse, along with owls and woodpeckers, live in the Bavarian forest. So, too, do lynx, which prey on the deer, and otters, which fish in the streams.

HISTORY

People have lived in Germany for many thousands of years. The Romans invaded in A.D. 9, but were forced back. From the 5th century, Germanic tribes called Franks conquered much of Europe. They became Christians.

In 843, the Frankish empire split, and from this split a German empire grew. But this in turn became divided into a number of separate states. In the 1600s Germany was torn apart by the Thirty Years War. In northeastern Germany, a strong kingdom called Prussia arose.

The Prussians helped defeat the French armies led by Napoleon. In 1871 the Prussian Chancellor Bismarck united Germany by a mixture of diplomacy and force.

When Germany entered World War I (1914–1918) against Britain and France, it was one of the world's strongest countries. But defeat left it in ruins. In 1933 Adolf Hitler became Germany's leader. He rebuilt Germany into a military state, and this led to World War II. Within Germany and its occupied lands, 16 million people, including Jews, Russians, Ukrainians, and prisoners of war, were killed. The killing of the Jews is known as the Holocaust.

In 1945 when Germany surrendered to the British, U.S., and Soviet armies, the country was divided. West Germany was a democracy. East Germany was a Communist state that was controlled by the USSR. In 1990 the two Germanies were united. Helmut Kohl became the first Chancellor (head of state) of the reunited Germany. Angela Merkel, Germany's first woman Chancellor, was elected in 2005.

LANGUAGE

German, like English, belongs to the group of languages known as Germanic. Throughout Germany, people speak Standard German (*Hochdeutsch*) as well as local dialects. German is also the official language of Austria and one of the official languages of Switzerland. Written German is the same everywhere. It is based on the language used by Martin Luther when he translated the Bible in the 16th century. You may see the letter "ß," which is pronounced "ss." German nouns begin with a capital letter.

Useful words and phrases

English	German
Zero	*null*
One	*eins*
Two	*zwei*
Three	*drei*
Four	*vier*
Five	*fünf*
Six	*sechs*
Seven	*sieben*
Eight	*acht*
Nine	*neun*
Ten	*zehn*
Sunday	*Sonntag*
Monday	*Montag*
Tuesday	*Dienstag*

Useful words and phrases

English	German
Wednesday	*Mittwoch*
Thursday	*Donnerstag*
Friday	*Freitag*
Saturday	*Samstag/ Sonnabend*
Good morning	*Guten Morgen*
Good-bye	*Auf Wiedersehen*
Please	*Bitte*
Thank you	*Danke*
How are you?	*Wie geht es Ihnen?*
Very well, thank you	*Sehr gut, danke*

INDEX

Acknowledgments
Book created for Highlights for Children, Inc. by Bender Richardson White.
Editors: Peter MacDonald and Lionel Bender
Designer: Malcolm Smythe
Art Editor: Ben White
Editorial Assistant: Madeleine Samuel
Picture Researcher: Madeleine Samuel
Production: Kim Richardson

Maps produced by Oxford Cartographers, England.
Banknotes from MRI Bankers Guide to Foreign Currency.
Stamps courtesy of Scott Publishing Co., Sidney, OH 45365 (www.scottonline.com).

Editorial Consultant: Andrew Gutelle
Germany Consultant: Ingrid Lenz-Aktas, Aschheim, Germany
Top Secret Guide to Germany has been produced with the help of German Consultant, Stefanie Teichmann, London.
Managing Editor, Highlights New Products: Margie Hayes Richmond

Picture Credits
DS = David Simson/DAS Photos. EU = Eye Ubiquitous. JD = James David Travel Photography. WK: = ©Wolfgang Kaehler, www.wkaehlerphoto.com. Z = Zefa.
t = top, b = bottom, r = right, l = left, c = center.
Cover: EU/Paul Thompson. Page 6-7: EU/JD. 7t, 7b: EU/David Cumming. 8l: EU/BB Pictures. 8-9: EU/JD. 9: EU/BB Pictures. 10: EU/ M. Barlow. 11t: EU/JD. 11b: Z/Streichan. 12t: Z/Haenel. 12b: Z. 12-13: WK. 14: DS. 15t: EU/JD. 15b: EU/J. B. Pickering. 16: Z/Waldkirch. 17t: EU. 17b: Courtesy of Mercedes Benz/Daimler-Chrysler, Inc. 18: EU/D. Cumming. 18-19: WK. 19t: Lionheart Books/BRW. 20: EU/D. Cumming. 21t: ©Friedhelm Holleczek. 21b: DS. 22: DS. 23l: DS. 23r: Z/Kinne. 24l: EU/Andrew Cudbertson. 24-25: Z/Damm. 25: DS. 26-27: Z/Damm. 27t: EU/John D. Norman. 26-27b: WK. 28: DS. 29: DS. 30 DS.

Illustration on page 1 by Tom Powers.